Unleashing the
Chief Moment Officers™

Reliably Giving the Gift of
Exceptional Experiences

Diane Serbin Hopkins
Certified Experience Economy Expert

Chicago, IL
www.networlding.com

DEDICATION

I am pleased to dedicate this book to the two most important Chief Moment Officers I've ever known.

My Dad Frank Serbin and my Mom Patricia Serbin.

Not only did they create a wonderful childhood for my sisters and I, filled with great moments that are forever happy memories, they both brought unique passion to build extraordinary moments for the customers they worked with through their careers. They like all parents were the first designers of exceptional experiences I ever knew.

Lucky for me I was watching closely!

ACKNOWLEDGEMENTS

I have been observing, teaching, developing ideas and gathering quotes to create this book over the past 5 years. I've had the privilege to be supported by smart and generous souls in my personal and professional life along the way and I'm happy to offer a brief acknowledgement of that support. Before I jump into the whole list, there are three men who opened my eyes to something I had been passionate about most of my life but didn't know it was called experience design.

My thanks to Joe Pine and Jim Gilmore who went beyond sharing their theories and expertise in books and launched a deeper dive certification program to build better understanding and tools around staging memorable experiences…And, they let me in their first class! This intensive learning opportunity opened up a whole new world for me. Also, I would never have had the opportunity to step into this world without the support of my mentor and partner in innovation, Phil Newbold. Thank you, thank you to my three personal Moment Masters!

I've been blessed to have many who care for me help me keep things moving and in balance and I'm forever grateful for their interest, enthusiasm and love. Although it's dangerous to list some and potentially leave out some, I must share my appreciation for the kindness and care given to me.

Thanks to...my husband Robert Hopkins, my son, Benjamin Stover, my mother Patricia Serbin, my late father, Frank Serbin, sisters, Joanne Losse and Carol Houck, and Franni Danowski, Sharon Bohn, Cindy Silver, Carol Struett, Corina Peacock, Dan Calista, Matt Krathwohl, David Kelly, Joel English, Lora Tatum, Evelyn Stover, Karen Oxler, Lara Lee, Mark Lavallee, MD, Cindy Mayfield, MD, Meg Heim, Valerie Willis, Teri Watson, PhD, Beth Peterson, Diane Bones, Sally Malik, Ellen and Allen Rogers, Sharon Dunn, Tinker Marshall, Martin Harris, MD, Maria Slager, Lori Allen, Dawn McCaskill, Chris Endres, Mike O'Neil, Gaylene Anderson, Kim Smoyer, Kim Saville, Ken Anderson, DO, Mark Tarner, Mark Wagner, Lauren McAteer, Adrienne Farnham, Joseph York, PhD, Monty Duke, MD, Melissa Wilson, Sue Neuffer, Maggie Scroope and Elaine Kauffman.

Yes, I am blessed!

TABLE OF CONTENTS

FOREWORD

I am excited to share with you the hopes, theories and observations I've gathered around the never-ending quest to make customers delighted repeat purchasers. Over the past 15 years I've had the privilege of being on the frontline of customer experience efforts within the healthcare industry and I've backed up my knowledge by studying many different businesses and different approaches to customer satisfaction and loyalty building. I've also been blessed to have been an eager student of some of the smartest business thinkers in the area of customer relations. I have a personal dream team of authors and experts that have influenced my theories and practice including: Phil Newbold, Tom Peters, Larry Keeley, Joe Pine, Jim Gilmore, Dev Patniak, the Late Sara Miller Caldicott and Joseph Michelli.

One theme resonated with me over my years of customer experience exploration: the idea that this work revolves around giving someone the gift of something extraordinary. It's an intangible but touching gift when someone goes beyond your expectations to meet your needs. It's a gift when a customer takes the time to tell you when you've failed miserably at meeting their needs instead of just never purchasing again, and it's a gift when staff members are well prepared and empowered to bring their best thinking, real-life insights and ideas forward to benefit the customer, patient, donor or investor.

I have seen companies that regularly exceed customer expectations and they often have a clear passion for staying relevant to customers and strive for consistency and clear communications. Much of this work centers around numbers, such as sales, satisfaction scores, customer research projects and market share. These numbers certainly drive strategy and offerings, but they can't always drive reliable behavior. The predictor of any company's ability to create exceptional experiences is talent: the people we choose to hire and retain, and whether or not each individual feels they have influence and their perspective and insights are valued. Of course, we bring our individual personalities to work with us, and some of those personalities complement customer interactions while others do not. Organizations committed to long-term exceptional experience relationships with their customers need to regularly and energetically prepare their teams with methods to build upon their individual strengths and genuinely care about their personal influence on each and every customer encounter.

This book is a summary of what I've found can re-ignite a passion for keeping the customer care promise primarily by observing ways to engage all staff. I have had the pleasure of working with thousands of healthcare professionals on customer experience planning and frequently I've seen staff who saw their job as just a paycheck but when given the opportunity to authentically contribute, transformed into pride-filled ambassadors of great service and positive attitudes. It's not about leaders determining what's right and handing it to workers to deliver. It's about the worm's eye view, (looking at where the rich soil is), and the bird's eye view, (looking at where priorities interconnect), coming together to for new levels of engagement and reliable results, due to the fact that there are so many moving parts as any enterprise sets out to delight their customers it can often feel overwhelming. By deliberately focusing on smaller steps on the way toward being extraordinary, the effort is more manageable. The focus on the moment allows each employee to connect with how they can influence customer satisfaction and "ultimately" company performance.

I trust that your perspective will expand and benefit from my observations. More importantly, I hope that you will find yourself ready to try some new approaches on the Monday morning after reading. I hope these concepts will drive experimentation and bolster courage to re-invent customer experience strategy by supporting all team members in any industry to create moments that matter. In keeping with this goal, I also hope that your interaction with the book is an exceptional experience. I have included easy-to-try approaches that may speed up your ability to test some new ideas into action. I've also included a collection of Chief Moment Officer truths based on my observations to help you along your path. If you complete the book you have the opportunity to personally accept your new role as a Chief Moment Officer. This new role will hopefully apply to your career as well as any volunteer activities. The guidelines for your virtual Moment Officer ceremony are provided and I strived to offer many opportunities to expand your thinking and experimentation. I always feel that when I discover new ways to frame or pursue a challenge, it's like receiving a gift. Thank you for desiring to find new ways to improve connections with your customers and for selecting *Unleashing the Chief Moment Officers* as part of your journey. You are certainly a gift to me!

Diane Serbin Hopkins

1

Never Underestimate the Difference a Moment Can Make

THE CONCEPT OF A MOMENT

One evening while dining with family, six year old Seth was wondering how long it would take for his macaroni and cheese dinner to arrive. At first his mother, Meaghan, reported it would probably be about 10 more minutes. When he asked again how much longer, she asked that he be patient for a moment. Sweet Seth thought a bit and then asked us all, "How many minutes is a moment?"

Although I thought I was just out for a relaxing dinner, I was then driven to think more about what a moment really is. The dictionary definition of a moment is a short interval of time, a particular instant or a significant time or occasion. But my experience design work was pulling me to deeper definitions. We've all used the word as a measurement in time—"Please wait a moment"—or as a way to identify something that stands out—"It was a boring movie but it had its moments." However, how often have we truly seen the power of a moment that changes how we feel, how we behave or how we buy?

Thinking more about the power of a Chief Moment Officer role, I now see moments as something that we experience internally. Not a measure of time, but more a measure of tenderness. Extraordinary customer experiences are made up of memorable moments of engagement that lead the customer or patient to feel valued, important and sometimes loved! An enterprise of CMO's isn't about getting the staff to smile or follow a mandatory script, it's about truly preparing the workforce to honor and apply their personal influence potential.

If this is how we envision a moment now, perhaps some new definitions are called for. Here are some descriptions of WHAT moments and Moment Officers can mean in a business:

Moment (noun): an interaction between people that evokes positive or negative feelings; a touchpoint between a person and a business or organization where expectations are met or missed. When seeking customer satisfaction or loyalty, moments can be thoughtfully designed to exceed customer expectations, anticipating their needs and creating loyalty and recommendation to others.

Do or Die Moments: While there are many exchanges between your staff, your website, your apps and your customers, not all moments carry the same weight. There are Do or Die Moments in any business that are non-negotiable, their importance doesn't change and the entire workforce needs to know what they are. These are the moments that must go well for customers or nothing else matters and they're typically core to why your company exists in the first place. The Geek Squad (one of my favorite service companies), can be as accessible as possible in the store, on-line and by phone but the Do or Die Moment is that they MUST be able to diagnose and fix my computer. A plumber can offer convenient 24 hour service but there must also be 24 hour access to the water heater I need. In the excitement of developing experience enhancement plans, companies must remember the core offering has to be fulfilled everytime.

Chief Moment Officer (noun): a direct or inferred role within a business where all associates are empowered and prepared to delight customers and they enthusiastically own this responsibility. The role exists in organizations with a culture of thoughtful anticipation and appreciation of customer desires and needs at all points in the customer journey. This shared role/responsibility exists so that the offerings are preferred, trust is built, and customers happily endorse the product or service.

Now for the WHY. Traditionally, delighting and exceeding customer expectations was pursued as a way to strengthen loyalty. However, in their book, *The Effortless Experience*, authors Matthew Dixon and Nick Toman share extensive customer research results and they report that "There is virtually no difference at all between the loyalty of those customers when expectations are exceeded and those who are simply met." One of the assumptions with this finding is that companies who go to great expense and effort to go from meeting to exceeding expectations are being wasteful. In this case, building a workforce of Chief Moment Officers is less about big spending and big effort, and more about aligned aspirations and attention to small influences and details, which don't present as much risk for waste. Also, despite these findings, there's still a need to meet expectations to build loyalty. There's also the potential impact when companies work to exceed customer's imagination. Exceeding imagination—giving customers perks, service or solutions they never dreamed of—is what this book is about. The goal is more than just customer loyalty. Other important benefits include:

- Having staff aligned to enthusiastically serve the customer and continually look for creative moments offers new levels of staff engagement and team building.

- An atmosphere that rewards and recognizes ever-expanding customer connections contributes to the "emotional" state of a company, or how ALIVE the company is, which helps with the recruitment and retention of great staff.

- The pursuit of great customer moments and impressions helps good companies stand out in the marketplace. More word-of-mouth promotion and differentiation, especially in the age of social media, helps move brands and offerings forward.

Other ways to define the Chief Moment Officer role for almost any business is to encourage these traits:

Solution Seeker. This is the best way to be ready for almost anything a customer may request or need. If you build a workforce of smart solution seekers and train them on how to find or get answers whenever they need them, moments will be mastered any day, any shift.

Therapist. This trait comes in very handy when customers have been seriously dissatisfied. Just as a psychologist offers a caring ear to a struggling patient, the CMO who can listen well, empathize and offer suggestions to improve the situation can often turn a customer from disgruntled to delighted.

Investigator. Being able to dig deeper to exceed expectations or turn around a moment gone bad is a valuable talent. Being aware of the difference between what customers say vs. what customers do can better prepare the company to stay in alignment with customer desires.

Mind Reader. This trait is really more about signal reading and tapping into what customers may be too shy or concerned to share. Experienced workers can sense patterns of confusion or needs and prepare accordingly. This is the trait that builds a culture of anticipation which makes customers feel highly valued. Over time, this becomes an instinct with high performing staff.

Surveyor. When company representatives are able to bridge the big picture (what the company promises) with the moment by moment picture (what this customer needs now), there's great opportunity to stay relevant and delight. Solid surveyor skills show an understanding that there is more at stake than the purchase at hand. Surveyors understand the reasons customers buy aren't all the same and at times it's important to look at the much bigger picture, which includes the customer's customer and beyond. In Business to Business companies, the customer's customer can involve many levels and a variety of associated needs.

Cheerleader. When the customer's taste or choices are affirmed, customers feel good about their purchase now and in the future. Having CMO's who are able to genuinely cheer on a customer for their excellent purchasing decisions help support the repeat purchasing and loyalty opportunities.

Tour Guide. A Chief Moment Officer should seek to live up to the lyrics of the Aladdin song, *A Whole New World* and offer "unbelievable sights, indescribable feeling…a wondrous place." Since many customers approach purchase decisions with trepidation, often expecting to be disappointed, striving to open up a whole new world of positive emotions can set the stage for a great ongoing relationship.

Dreamer. Having a vivid imagination and interest in creating better and better experiences allows an individual and a company to move beyond what's expected. This inspired approach can make all the difference in being ordinary or extraordinary. Delighting those who pay your salary should involve imagination, and should be approached as a quest to swell the hearts of those you serve.

Knight in Shining Armor. When our well-intentioned systems fail customers, leading them to be stuck in a company maze or to endure repeated dissatisfiers, all can be saved when attentive staff are prepared to save the day, or the moment. Service recovery or failure identification with care can turn things around when things go bad. Unfortunately, there are days when customers must be rescued from how our policies, procedures or bad hires make them feel.

Apology Experts. Apologies are important to change the direction of hurt feelings or broken promises in any business. Dr. Gary Chapman is a best-selling author of books such as *The Five Love Languages* on marriage enrichment. He stresses that not only do people have different love languages, individuals have different needs for apologies to be meaningful. I see applications on how husbands and wives need to thoughtfully tend to apologies and how companies need to prepare the workforce to apologize. Dr. Chapman and Dr. Jennifer Thomas wrote a book, *The Five Languages of Apology* that explains apology dimensions such as regret, taking responsibility and offering restitution. Chief Moment Officers need to study customers and customer reactions to be able to match the type of apology to the needs of that customer. One size doesn't likely fit all when it comes to customer apologies. Exceptional experience companies should offer staff a variety of approved approaches.

Gift Givers. In many situations it can be better to give than receive and a Chief Moment Officer company needs to be aligned to allow staff to see this come true. Having an enthusiastic giving heart at work is a great start for a successful career and contribution in any position. Once the gift giving approach is in place, having clear guidance on what aligns with customer needs and desires and competitive issues will lead to customers receiving more than they expected.

THE PURSUIT OF EXCEPTIONAL MOMENTS

The path to great satisfaction from my observations must be lined with good, great and extraordinary moments. For a successful journey, it's important that every enterprise invest time and energy to prepare their workforce to never waste a chance to delight a customer. The next step, where leaders take a fresh look at customer service strategies and policies, is crucial. Many companies pursue this through various types of customer journey mapping and in some situations, this offers great insight and in others it's not deep enough to uncover new ways to care for customers. Beyond scripting, complaint management and minimally-inspiring customer service training, there is a micro-level to explore. By zooming into moment by moment interactions there's a fresh opportunity to delight customers and to strengthen the customer-focused culture overall. The desired outcome from all of the moment mastery recommended in this book is a word that has many different meanings...DELIGHT. My definition of the word Delight, as it's connected to the role of a Chief Moment Officer is that it's a tremendously pleasurable state that comes about when a company deliberately acts to design customer experiences that recognize and accommodate the stated or unstated desires of customers. Author and customer service expert Shep Hyken speaks about a progression of customer contacts including Moments of Truth, Moments of Misery, Moments of Mediocrity and Moments of Magic. Unfortunately every company offers up mediocre and misery moments at some point. The hope is that by building a workforce of Chief Moment Officers, the mediocre and misery moments will be drastically reduced. Companies should not underestimate the power of going *small*.

One of my favorite customer experience thought leaders is Bruce Temkin founder of the Temkin Group. His free e-book, The Six Laws of Customer Experience, includes the concept that "Every interaction creates a personal reaction." As employees become better prepared to create exceptional moments one customer at a time, the company gains competitive advantage. The pursuit of a Chief Moment Officer culture helps build collective knowledge of how different customers have different needs, feelings and desires. In order to accommodate these differences and prompt positive customer reactions, I recommend four core experience design concepts:

Personalize: try to tailor offerings, access and communication.

De-Mystify: don't allow customers to stay confused or lost whenever they interact with your organization.

Humanize: be attentive to customer sensitivities and restrictions and strive to find ways to build confidence and comfort.

Safety-Check: as new ideas are generated to enhance the customer journey, be sure to always pre-check possible safety implications for customers and workers.

One of the first references to the *small things matter* theory was the book, Moments of Truth, written in 1987. Jan Carlzon was the CEO of Scandinavian Airlines and he believed that, "every interaction with a customer was the basis on which the entire organization could be judged." His approaches to aligning the organization around service to the customers was an impressive business turnaround lesson. An important way to accelerate passion for customer experience in an organization is to promote an atmosphere of team members *Feeling Ownership AND Taking Ownership*. This can happen when small things are pursued to build customer confidence and loyalty. It's a reminder of the Biblical lesson in Proverbs 3:27: "Do not withhold good from those to whom it is due when it is within your power to do so." Of course, leaders have to relinquish some power so staff can do what's needed.

There are those who believe that working to exceed customer expectations is really just a way to set your company up for ultimate failure, since raising the bar requires continual raising of the bar to eventually, an unsustainable level. In many cases, just meeting customer expectations is seen as exceptional in the eyes of a customer. We have all had many unsatisfying experiences, so when a company actually does what they promise, many customers are thrilled. Rather than worry about the baseline of customer satisfaction being too high in the long-term, think more about guarding against *Moments that Disappoint* while repeating *Moments that Delight*. Delighting is different for each customer, and sometimes *meeting expectations* is delightful to one where *exceeding expectations* is delightful for others. To continue to differentiate your brand and compete in an increasingly competitive marketplace, consider striving to build opportunities to *exceed imagination*. That's an extra-credit approach that builds not only repeat business, but excitement and new levels of relevancy. Exceeding a customer's imagination can be achieved when you look beyond what they've told you they need or want. Take the time to look deeper at how you meet their current or expected needs and anticipate what else they may need before or after your interaction. Searching to build unexpected solutions to expand your relevancy can be extremely satisfying to customers and extremely satisfying to staff, who become re-energized about expanding their contributions.

"We don't remember days, we remember moments."

— Ceasar Pavese

The Chief Moment Officer is a role that should be part of every worker's job description. It's the exciting opportunity for every person to contribute their best attitude, their best knowledge, and their best accommodation of needs for someone trusting the company with their purchasing power. For this role to be embraced and adequately fulfilled, business leaders must value moments and build accountabilities so that everyone's "inner moment officer" can thrive.

One of the first lenses workers must consider is what's typically referred to as being open to serving. Having a servant's heart is the basis for a variety of management books. Pastor Tom Fries shared a lesson from his childhood that struck me as a great reminder of how those of us with customers need to think about our roles as Chief Moment Officers. He told us that his Grandmother used to teach a lesson to her grandsons by saying, *"Maybe it's time for you to take off the bib and put on the apron."* That simple quote reminded me of how many times I've seen people in companies I shop at either wearing aprons (enthusiastically serving customers), or wearing bibs (looking for ways to meet their own needs). As we explore the power of building a workforce of Chief Moment Officers, we must also keep in mind how our companies are organized for the benefit of the customer or comfort of the worker, as there are times when both can be achieved, but not always. In addition to the concepts outlined in the coming chapters on how customer moments should be thoughtfully designed, remember to check out the policies, procedures and strategies in place that may make it hard for an enthusiastic Chief Moment Officer to offer extraordinary experiences to those who drive revenue.

Some specific steps businesses should consider to prepare to unleash the Chief Moment Officers are:

- Consistent and dynamic educational offerings about customer needs and moment mastery, not just satisfaction scores, should be part of regular operations.

- Leaders and staff should always be looking inside and outside of the industry for great consumer experience lessons that can be applied.

- Policies and procedures must continually be reviewed to see if they present barriers to customer needs or desires.

- Those in charge need to regularly try out the company experience to see what they may be missing. (Think Undercover Boss)—this should include the web experience, mobile experience, onsite or in-person experience, phone experience, etc.

- Upon on-boarding and throughout the work year, leaders must demonstrate and recognize the key role every worker can play in delighting customers.

- Staff must see regular personal reminders of the impact they can have.

- Hiring and retention strategies must include ways to recruit and retain staff who care about customer needs and desires and the benefits that come when customers are well cared for.

- Staff should feel encouraged by their employer so they can feel confident to continually look for new ways to engage with customers.

- Abundant sharing of great customer moments to repeat will help spread the effort company-wide.

As a company embraces this perspective, DELIGHTFUL MOMENTS will lead to the DESIRED MOMENTUM toward <u>reliable</u> extraordinary experiences. If a renewed commitment to exceptional experiences begins without full support from leaders, it could be just another passing program.

DELIGHTFUL MOMENTS **TO** **DESIRED MOMENTUM**
One Customer Interaction   A Customer Passionate
At a Time   Organization

"It's nice to be important but it's more important to be nice."

— Anonymous

Taking the time and effort to assess the current state of worker customer experience training, goal and accountability alignment and ongoing recognition of great efforts will keep this from being just another priority. Ultimately businesses should seek to progress along this continuum:

RELIABLE CUSTOMER EXPERIENCE CULTURE JOURNEY

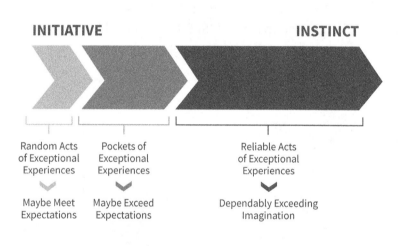

WHY FOCUSING DOWN TO THE MOMENT MATTERS IN BUSINESS

No matter the business or offering, staying viable and meaningful to customers is more complex than ever. There is a perfect storm of conditions now in place that have raised exceptional customer experiences to the level of core business strategy. Based on common customer dissatisfaction indexes, for some this commonsense concept hasn't been a core business strategy for a variety of reasons. The issues and influences are big, and many companies respond only in big ways. Focusing on moments can be a zig strategy where others zag and it's about engaging the entire organization to embrace the difference almost anyone can make.

Many workers see nurturing a customer service strategy as something too big to personally influence, and focus on the bigger decisions of pricing, packaging, distribution, training and policies. All of these things certainly can make or break a customer's experience, and many big issues matter. However, every single worker can find their direct influence when there's more of a focus on making key moments, key interactions, and key touch points the best they can be. One moment at a time, one person at a time is something most people can master and wrap their minds around and an important way to stand out from competitors.

"Every moment is a fresh beginning."

— T.S. Elliot

The following graph illustrates some of the most important aspects supporting a refreshed and comprehensive customer experience strategy. The first compelling reason

Constantly Connected Consumer Feedback via Social Media

Speed of Concept to Market via Technology

COMPELLING REASONS TO COMMMIT TO EXCEPTIONAL CUSTOMER MOMENTS

Unique & Disruptive Competition Facing Most Businesses

Commoditization in Many Industries

Need for Customer Retention Loyalty ROI

is the constant connection and the purchasing power influence social media presents. When customers have the ability to quickly and broadly share what they like or hate about a service or product, businesses must be prepared to fuel positive endorsements. Next is the almost daily waves of disruptive competition coming from both traditional and unlikely competitors. Uber is a perfect example of how whole new models can surface, causing traditional companies to rethink their customer connections. Another compelling issue is the commoditization trap facing many industries, where it gets harder and harder for customers to differentiate between one product or service and another. Most enhancements to products or services can be copied quickly, but exceptional customer experiences offered by every staff member and at every contact point can be difficult for competitors to replicate. In addition, advances in all types of customer-facing technology are increasing quickly, but strong customer relationship strategies can help combat the competitive force of the new technology options. Finally, retaining existing customers is much less expensive than always looking for new customers. A strong, thoughtful customer connection strategy can help transform satisfied customers to a sales force of raving fans.

"Your customers are only satisfied because their expectations are so low and because no one else is doing better. Just having satisfied customers isn't good enough anymore. If you really want a booming business, you have to create Raving Fans."

— Ken Blanchard

CONSTRUCTS OF MEANINGFUL, MAGNIFICENT MOMENTS:

Your organization likely has existing frameworks to enhance customer service and they may change over the years based on the market or changes in leadership. In some companies core principles for customer service stay in place as an anchor. Mark Tarner, President of the South Bend Chocolate Company in Indiana built a thriving restaurant and candy enterprise from a single family recipe. He shared that he believes extraordinary customer experiences are very similar to great employee engagement. He said, "Customers want to do business with companies they Respect, Love and Trust and workers want to be part of companies they Respect, Love and Trust." Mark and his leaders work to prepare teams to understand these concepts as a foundation for the big and little customer experience decisions they make.

The way extraordinary moments are defined for a thriving customer centered culture will depend upon the type of business you're in, the type of customers you serve, and the past successes and failures your organization has experienced over its history. The following is a collection of moment-framing behaviors to help build your Magnificent Moment definitions for your company.

EXERCISE: *Select the top 10 words that you feel best align with what your customers need from their relationship with your company and share this with colleagues to see if their choices align with yours.*

Chief Moment Officers may wish to master:

Empathy	Hospitality	Anticipation	Kindness
Attentiveness	Serving	Sharing	Admiring
Comforting	Welcoming	Generosity	Honor
Hosting	Flexibility	Openness	Sharing
Teaching	Guiding	Protecting	Listening
Sensing	Organize	Warmth	Expecting
Assure	Reassure	Soothe	Secure
Easing	Relieve	Encourage	Cheer
Understand	Fulfilling	Attend	Aid
Steering	Escort	Nudge	Confer
Surprise	Console	Encourage	Nurture
Inclusion	Tutoring	Advising	Charm

WHAT CHIEF MOMENT OFFICERS AREN'T

If the concept of having an enterprise-wide brigade of Chief Moment Officers offers new promise for how your customer engagement strategies could be strengthened, it's important to think a bit about what this role isn't. Building an enterprise of customer centered teams brings some boundaries that need to be managed. Chief Moment Officers are not meant to be:

Renegades: Having a company filled with Chief Moment Officers doesn't mean it's wild west time. Creative solutions are welcome but disruptions to smooth operations are not. Efforts to delight customers must be practical and within rules and regulations. Although it may be tempting to try anything, it should only stretch some procedures, not break them. Grand gestures are great, but must be respectful of well-designed systems.

Conditionally Accommodating: The sub-title of this book is: *Reliably Giving the Gift of Exceptional Experiences*…emphasis on the word *reliably*. Customers need to become accustomed to a level of service, care or assistance no matter who may be working, the time of day, the location, etc. The night shift at a 24 hour pharmacy has to be just as knowledgeable and prepared as the day shift. Insurance companies need to be just as responsive to customers who have a crash in the winter as those who do in the summer. Reliable levels of delight need to be woven into the culture of an organization so that customer loyalty and satisfaction are just as reliable.

Unproductive: Whether you're part of a business with 10 staff members or a workforce of 40,000, there are similar needs for engaging well with customers and protecting precious productivity and effective operations. Some team members may be natural customer connectors and are dependable in meeting customer expectations, however, the extra time they may take to delight a customer may be in conflict with the real-world efficiencies needed to stay in business. This is not a case of either/or but of both/and. Productive operations and connectivity to customers must be balanced. This is especially true in call centers where too much time nurturing one customer on the phone leads to more on-hold time for other customers. Call abandonment rates are bad for business, so again, balance is the key.

Transactional Ticket Takers: CMO's are not on auto-pilot. Companies that embrace the thoughtful and deliberate design of exceptional experiences can't simply look at customer contacts as transactions that fuel revenue. A workforce of CMO's will not tolerate mundane interactions but will strive for a focus on a customer journey and relationships. There needs to be no such thing as a routine customer contact.

Smothering: In many customer relationships it's ok to offer a bit of Mothering but no Smothering. Sometimes companies build such enthusiasm and even a competitive spirit around serving customers that some staff go over the edge and attack the customer with knowledge, care and attention. We've all had a shopping experience where the salesperson greeted us as we entered the store, asked how they could help and seemed to then follow us around at every moment waiting to almost pounce on our next question or need. Being hovered over is rarely comfortable and being smothered with too much attention can turn the best of intentions into a dissatisfying experience.

Takers: As a company prepares staff to be great customer engagers, an old lesson applies... Never take more than you give... A "taker" mentality is a barrier to a customer centric culture. Workers who abruptly stop an interaction with a customer to take a break, or who only provide answers to direct questions instead of generously sharing context and supplemental information are not "givers". We can't expect to take the customer's money, take their trust and loyalty, take their valuable time and give back the minimum service. Teams must be made up of members who give the attention, time, knowledge and care beyond the transaction at hand.

Chapter I
Key Learning Moments I Want to Act Upon:

———————————————

II

It All Begins & Ends with Talent (and Systems)

Hiring and Grooming Chief Moment Officers

The people we choose to hire and retain in our companies are the foundation of a sustainable enterprise and successful relationship-building with customers. It's important to know whether or not each person feels they have any influence on the big issues and priorities, and if they feel their insights and reactions are valued. Of course we all bring our individual personalities to work with us and some of those personalities complement customer interactions while others do not. Businesses committed to long-term exceptional experiences for their customers need to regularly and energetically infuse their teams with examples of how to build on individual strengths and authentically recognize their personal influence on each customer encounter.

There are places within every company where customers consistently receive exceptional attention without any clear strategy or training. That's the *LUCK OF THE HIRE* approach, which is not sustainable and certainly not consistent enough to build a company culture around.

HIRING

There is an abundance of research available to support best hiring practices. There are so many issues to consider, depending upon the industry. Whatever the traditional or recommended hiring practices may be, I'd like to suggest one more consideration to add to the mix. When filling new positions, are you prepared to hire people who have a light on inside? Are you able to see and feel a spark in their eyes or an engaged heart? All the online surveys or resumes in the world won't give you this information. To add the customer experience lens to your recruitment efforts, especially for positions dealing directly with customers, consider developing screening approaches to help you search for that "light." The goal is to see if they shine with you to predict how they might shine with your customers.

Here are some methods to consider adding to your hiring practices to find Chief Moment Officer types:

1. Aim High. As you review the hiring process, keep in mind the famous aspirations in Jim Collin's book *From Good to Great.* Jim said, "People are not your most important asset, the RIGHT people are." Why on earth should you settle for just good team members? Keep your eyes set on finding great employees with great energy, great compassion and great attention to detail. Also aim high as you look at your existing workforce. Never underestimate the hidden star performers in various roles or departments. As new projects come up or new customer efforts are launched, have an open casting call for people who may be excited about the issue. Maintain a culture where people feel safe offering their perspective and perspiration and you will identify some great contributors who have been hidden by their managers or by company policies and culture.

2. Don't interview candidates, audition them. Many companies are now learning more about how a candidate can shine when placed next to other candidates vying for a new position. Group interview sessions allow you to see who is the most self-assured and comfortable with surprises. With 2-4 candidates in the room responding to important scenarios, you'll be able to observe who rises to the occasion and shines.

3. Ask candidates how they complain. When interviewing include some questions to discover what type of customer they are when interacting with a company by having them share complaints they've had with companies in the past. This exercise will give you an indication of how observant they are and about how they think customers should be served in general. You will also begin to get a sense of their passion level. The desired outcome for this method is to see if they can articulate dissatisfying situations in a respectful way and if they take the time to propose a suggested fix. If they do, they may be well suited to do the same for your customers.

"Kindness begets kindness."

— Greek Philosophy

4. Search for Likeabilty. Likeability is incredibly underestimated, yet it's a core way to determine how we interact with those around us. It's difficult to ascertain who might be likeable to one type of person in comparison to another type. However, the fundamentals of likeabilty include approachability, openness, and positivity.

Your goal is to find staff with natural charm. Charm in this case is the ability to give delight or prompt admiration. People are generally likeable when they are non-threatening, cheerful, and appear genuinely interested in their job and those around them. They encourage customers to talk about their situations and they actually listen. Overall, likeable people offer a refreshing, positive pause in the day. As you interview candidates, add a likeability lens during conversations and see if you're left with a sense that they provided you with a positive pause in your day.

5. Safety as an Engager. You can probe a bit about someone's perspective on maintaining a safe environment for workers and customers to judge how likely they would be to help others feel well cared for. Guarding customers and co-workers from harm and taking safety seriously can be another indicator of a great, caring, and engaged contributor. Special moments can come when a restaurant hostess checks to see if a single woman wants an escort to her car at night, or when a hotel clerk insists on lifting the luggage of a pregnant customer. Showing customers the extra attention to their personal safety prompts a sense of feeling truly appreciated which is a core concept for Chief Moment Officers!

6. Uncover Emotional Intelligence. When you are recruiting well-trained, experienced, solid-thinking new team members, don't forget to also look for those who can think and feel at a higher level. There are a variety of Emotional Intelligence surveys or scenarios to incorporate into the hiring process to offer another layer of protection against Low Customer Experience candidates.

"Some people lead for a lifetime, others receive only a moment to show the way."

— John Maxwell

Many prospective employees dread the orientation process. They expect boring hours of policy and procedure review and consider the experience a necessary evil of sorts in order to begin their new position. However, if you want to set your well-hired staff members up for customer service success, consider the on-boarding process as your Chief Moment Officer boot camp and walk the talk by striving to delight each new employee.

The key to "wowing" your new staff members and properly preparing them for great customer interactions ahead boils down to one design principle:

Make them feel IMPORTANT!

The goal of the new employee orientation needs to be that every staff member goes home afterward and says:

"You won't believe what they did for us, today!"

For us, not *to* us. While attending orientation programs, the participants should continue to think, *"All this for me?"*

Essentially, you need to deliberately create an experience where new recruits have positive stories to share with their family and friends that relate to feeling valued, feeling inspired, and feeling that their views are important to leaders. Orientation is where that sense of pride begins. Purposely incorporate pride-filled content or moments whenever possible as a model for moments to come.

"Hiring the best is your most important task."

— Steve Jobs

Some exceptional on-boarding concepts to consider:

1. Have executive staff or owners greet new staff as part of the on-boarding. When "Big Bosses" show up, looking staff members in the eye and shaking their hands, it creates a great memory and story to tell. Servant leaders can go even further by helping to serve beverages as well as offering to field direct questions. Seeing that leaders believe new staff orientations are important commitments leaves a great first impression.

2. Create signature moments during the training that display how staff connect to the company and its mission in memorable ways. Share grand stories of organizational achievements, build understanding about the history, distribute unexpected gifts. If possible, find fun ways for the newbies to bond and prepare to support each other during their learning curves. Prepare a string of moments to assist them with a successful entry into the organization and successful connecting with customer needs.

3. Check the general tone of the orientation process. Is the overall tone to welcome the new staff one of "You all are lucky you made it into this great company," or, hopefully, "We're so excited you chose to join our team?" The attitude toward the newest members of the team sets a tone for the future that will surely influence customer service positioning, so ensure that the attitudes shown as people enter the organization are as fully welcoming and appreciative as possible.

4. Sow the seeds of Pride. This may be easier or harder depending upon what type of company you're in. However, you can use emotional videos or in-person storytelling to illustrate the great performance achieved around your company. Share impressive recognition stories, customer feedback, and plans for the future as much as possible so the valuable seeds of pride are planted. Overall don't leave the first impressions of the company to chance but instead deliberately present reasons each new worker can become a raving fan.

"A customer is the most important visitor on our premises, he is not dependent on us. We are dependent on him or her. He is not an interruption in our work. He is the purpose of it. He is not an outsider in our business. He is part of it. We are not doing him a favour by serving him. He is doing us a favour by giving us an opportunity to do so."

— Mahatma Ghandi

ALIGNING

One of the most important aspects of connecting the people of the company to the people who purchase from the company is making sure those who are hired to take good care of the customer are aligned to that task. This alignment process can often begin with what titles are used for jobs. One of the first steps to understanding what you do is what knowing what your job is called, and what that implies.

Many years ago Disney set an important standard by sharing with the world that every staff member at Disney, no matter what their actual duties are, is a "Cast Member." Thomas Allin, the first Chief Veteran's Experience Officer at the VA found this to be a crucial factor as he explored roles and responsibilities of VA staff. He stated in a speech, "If I'm a scheduler, a customer is an interruption. If I'm a caregiver, the customer is whom I'm here for," he said. "The focus on the employees is clearly the biggest thing we have to do." This concept has also been adopted as a customer experience priority at the Cleveland Clinic, where all staff members have the title of "Caregiver" no matter where they work.

Consider taking a look at how well aligned titles may be to the desired influence for customers. I worked with one cafeteria operation that was struggling with customer satisfaction issues. As we looked deeper into the operations we discovered that the servers and cashiers in the cafeteria all shared the title of Food Service Clerk or Food Service Cashier. These titles may have been technically satisfying for the human resource team however they weren't well aligned to how each role should connect to the offerings and the customers. When interviewing the staff we found they saw themselves having little influence on the customer experience and felt of little importance within the structure of the company. As we worked to co-create a refreshed overall experience that focused more on the quality of the food and the interactions with staff, the need to re-visit titles was apparent. Once we determined that the promise to customers was not about just grabbing food and finding a seat but more about a true dining experience, and we learned that customers had questions about ingredients, calories, allergies, etc., we worked with the frontline staff to better align their roles and titles to exceptional experience aspirations. The new titles for both the servers and cashiers became Delicious Dining Experts. We supported the title change with new badges, personalized aprons and training to be sure they could live up to the name. Staff members were very appreciative of the attention, of the invitation to participate in the process and customer satisfaction improved.

In addition to the titles, compensation, rewards, and peer recognition all need to be tied to meaningful customer experiences. It's not unusual for customer satisfaction scores to drive some compensation and bonuses and awards. However, this can lead to intermittent results instead of a consistent culture. Consider ongoing checks of job descriptions and staff performance reviews to be sure that current customer needs and desires are well represented. If these processes are rarely revised, there can easily be an unintended lack of customer-focus and alignment.

"No one is useless in this world who lightens the burdens of another."

— Mark Twain

IT ALSO BEGINS AND ENDS WITH SYSTEMS

Although the quality of the talent is the most important factor in any organization, if even the most passionate performers are placed in poorly designed or ineffective systems, the systems will eventually extinguish that light. It's important to step back and regularly scan accepted practices that can be cumbersome or downright stupid, and may diminish the ability to delight customers. Rewards or reprimands must be consistent and make it clear that great service isn't optional. Since long-term employees often develop norms that may include customer-unfriendly systems, it's helpful to regularly have fresh eyes look at what's in place that could be improved. It's easy to unconsciously gravitate toward systems that may make life more comfortable for staff but fail the customer. Although every industry is different, you may begin your investigation of systems that block magnificent customer moments including: payment systems, hours of operations systems, customer feedback and inquiry systems, and distribution systems.

In his book, *The Milkshake Moment*, author Steven Little writes, "Well-intended systems meant to increase satisfaction can often produce the opposite effect for customers and employees." He shares important lessons on how to build breakthrough customer service seeking that precise instant in which an organization's individuals realize that they are allowed to do the right thing.

Some examples of ways to keep organizational systems from sabotaging exceptional experiences:

- Are your hours of operation in line with customer needs or changing needs?

- Do you have flexibility in staffing to accommodate traditionally high customer demand days or times?

- Do staff members know they will be supported when they work around systems to address important customer needs?

- When you promote benefits for customers, be sure those benefits are deliverable every time.

- For web-based customer transactions constantly check that sites work the way it's supposed to every time.

- Double check that some systems meant to prevent manipulation by untrustworthy customers (the 1%) don't make life difficult for your trustworthy loyal customers. In addition to checking the steps customers must take to buy from you, also note the general tone of voice.

"Systems run the business and people run the systems."

— Michael Gerber

MOMENT CENTERED TRAINING

Alignment of the overall customer service strategy requires regular, dynamic training and behavior accountability. One requirement for Chief Moment Officer training is to design customer experience training that is exceptional for each worker. Customer experience training time must include an engaging presentation of aspirations and techniques, create positive memories, and make each attendee feel valued, and like a true insider. This is a great time to fight the potential growth of an "us vs. them" syndrome that can grow within a company culture.

"Train staff to take responsibility for reaching customer service goals and create a secure working environment that fosters flexibility and innovation."
— Jan Carlzon

Some customer experience training program design principles to consider:

1. The Welcome is Really Welcoming. Instead of a mundane file into the room to prepare for a class, create some fun interactivity to help staff feel really welcomed not just for showing up, but for bringing their energy and knowledge to the discussion. Make it easy for staff to meet new co-workers and build cross-departmental connections and communication.

2. Leader Modeling. When those who often seem unreachable or detached from the customers share their views and interest, the experience overall becomes more important in the eyes of all participants. Include videos or presentations where senior leaders share ways they've participated in understanding and exceeding customer experiences.

3. Live Story-Telling of Great Customer Interactions. Including actual customers or other co-workers with great stories to tell will help contribute to the dynamic memories and understanding of all the ways it is possible to delight a customer.

4. Participative Ideation To Encourage Big Thinking. Although there will always be some prescriptive sharing, make sure to be open to ideas from all participants that can continue to refine the customer experience as you search to create raving fans.

5. Above Expectations Refreshments and Food. When staff are invited to workshops, a nice selection of food, snacks, and beverages where they're sure to find something that satisfies their tastes is a nice supplement to the learning. Simple touches like unexpected hospitality help staff feel special and can serve as a lesson in experiences that delight.

6. An Upbeat Exit. Ending the training with a sense of optimism, sincere appreciation, and clear direction on how to continually contribute ideas will help fuel positive memories and application of all that was learned. Be sure to create a fond farewell.

"You have to develop the discipline of momentarily blotting out the rest of the world. Believe me: your guests will know immediately when you've succeeded."

— Patrick O' Connell, Chef at the Inn at Little Washington

ENGAGING ALL TYPES

Many of the ideas described in this chapter apply perfectly to actual employees of an organization. There are important considerations to build ownership of moments depending upon the type of worker you may be leading. A few segments to pay special attention to are:

Contracted or Outsourced Workers: Customers typically don't care about the contractor or free-lance status of someone representing your organization. Despite contractors not having an actual employed status or stock ownership, they need to feel fully included and valued as part of the team driven to delight customers.

Long-term vs. New Staff: The length of time someone has been with a company may impact their attitudes about new approaches. In order to make the most of the knowledge base of long-term staff while being open to the fresh perspectives of new staff, be sure to acknowledge these differences as moment mastery strategies are pursued. Although the reasons to experiment are universal, methods to build adoption and enthusiasm may have to be tailored to the type of employees.

All Stars: In every company there are natural stars. These are people who have a warmth, energy, and the flexibility to do whatever it takes to satisfy the customer. They are great role models for other team members and you can almost always depend upon them. As you seek to strengthen the enterprise-wide support of moments leading to new customer service momentum, be sure not to take these high performers for granted. Consider having them help build out the framework and the training or have them lead the way in sharing "What worked" stories.

"It is not the employer who pays the wage. Employers only handle the money. It is the customer who truly pays the wages."

— Henry Ford

REMINDER STRATEGIES

There are companies that have great resources, strong staff engagement and loyalty, yet struggle with exceptional customer satisfaction or business performance. Some leaders scratch their heads wondering what could be preventing their well-trained, well-prepared and hopefully, well- hired teams from delivering exceptional customer moments most of the time. One simple explanation is that often people are so busy and distracted, they sometimes forget how little things can mean so much. One solution is to develop a deliberate Reminder Strategy for customer focused culture-building. Most people want to do their best but sometimes life gets in the way. One way to keep the mastery of the moment alive in the hearts and minds of the workforce is to offer extraordinary experience reminders. This helps to regularly remind a busy, distracted staff about who they're ultimately serving and how important their influence is on the company's reputation. Every company culture is different so use whatever internal communications channels have proven best for your structure, and make sure the messages are clear, heart-felt and bold. Whether you develop a full campaign supported by break room posters, inspiring videos, story-telling events, or mobile phone customer engagement texts, keep the every-person has impact connection a priority.

JC Penney and Macy's are examples of companies that have team member messaging around customer experience aspirations. One quote on a reminder display I observed in my Macy's proclaimed: "If everyone leaves our store feeling better for having come in, we have worked our magic." Other reminders that were on display near the dressing rooms included: smile, be kind, be helpful, be you!

Some options for a Reminder Strategy include:

- Posters in Backstage Staff Locations that reconnect team members with the customer. Consider headings such as WHO WILL YOU DELIGHT TODAY? Include compelling photography of customers or actual customers. Or, WHAT MASTERPIECE MOMENT HAVE YOU GIVEN A CUSTOMER TODAY THAT YOU WANT TO SIGN YOUR NAME TO? This one could be a simple empty frame, leaving what a beautiful moment might be up to their imagination.

- Inspiring Customer Experience Quotes. Post them in staff newsletters, share them at meetings, include them in training sessions.

- Customer Care Value Sharing. To truly align customer focus as a daily activity, consider a reminder strategy that has every meeting beginning with a core customer appreciation lesson. Encourage people to share lessons learned or effective strategies as a quick reminder of what's important. By doing this at every meeting, the importance of customer moments becomes clear.

"An individual without information can't take responsibility. An individual with information can't help but take responsibility."

— Jan Carlzon

KEY STEPS IN LAUNCHING A MOMENT MASTERY STRATEGY

A logical progression to launch a department or enterprise-wide Chief Moment Officer culture involves five key steps:

1. AWARENESS: take the time to clearly communicate to all staff the expectations around their personal influence and impact as Chief Moment Officers or customer caring partners.

2. UNDERSTANDING: develop systems to be sure that staff understand how to act upon the expectations that they are customer caring partners in the organization. Offer ongoing clarification of expected approaches or behaviors. Understanding can be enhanced by simple statements such as:

Guide Them With Grace, Pretend the Customer is Your Grandmother, Never End a Conversation Until You Know All Questions are Answered, Affirm the Customer's Decision to Contact Us Even If They Aren't Prepared to Buy.

3. PREPARE: insure that staff can deliver moments well through ongoing thoughtful and memorable training as well as leader role-modeling.

4. REMIND & REFINE: a commitment to nurture and support Chief Moment Officers never ends just as the quest to obtain and retain customers never ends. As the organization learns ways customers are delighted, refine systems and offerings to incorporate these lessons.

5. RECOGNIZE: test and implement bold sharing of Chief Moment Officer behaviors to build enthusiasm. Each company has recognition systems and traditions that support the current culture. Look for ways to honor recognition efforts that have been well received and find new ways to build visibility of high performers and effective approaches. Individual or group reward systems may work in some cultures or not in others.

Some companies can bring the happy customer in to celebrate the exceptional customer care. Choose recognition efforts that help turn moments into service momentum.

"Don't count the days. Make the days count."

— Muhammed Ali

Chapter II
Key Learning Moments I Want to Act Upon:

———————————————————

III

Appreciate the Gifts Customers Give...

Ranting and Raving

In addition to formal customer satisfaction survey tools or feedback channels, it's important to develop ways for staff to vividly understand why customers may be happy or sad. One of the most valuable gifts a customer can give your organization, (besides lots of repeat business), is a detailed description of how you are failing to meet their needs or how they engage with your service or products in ways you may not have expected. Whether it's through detailed review of survey comments, personal interviews or observational research, you can prepare the workforce to be the best Chief Moment Officers they can be by encouraging everyone to see customer complaints, feedback and requests as a gift! Anthony Ulwick, CEO of the consulting firm Stratgyn, offered important advice for companies as they listen to the voice of their customers when he said, "Treat discovered opportunities as sacred."

"Your customer doesn't care how much you know until they know how much you care."

— Damon Richards

SOME WAYS TO APPRECIATE CUSTOMER INSIGHT GIFTS...

1. Understand the work-arounds. Although our offerings are designed to be consumed and purchased for certain needs, customers may have other thoughts. Watch how customers interact with your products or services to see if any work-arounds have developed. Some work-arounds involve customers having to manipulate your cumbersome operations. This is evident whenever you see customers lining up early at the door of a merchant since obviously product availability or pricing can't be counted on all day long. Another common work-around is when airline passengers purchase round-trip tickets when they only need the outbound leg of the trip but it's too expensive to purchase alone. Other work-arounds are when customers find unintended value for your product or service. One of my favorite examples of a work-around or re-imagining of an offering is why people who don't own a cat purchase kitty litter. Some buy this product to help get traction when driving in the snow. Don't limit your understanding of a customer's relationship with your organization or products to what they tell you, look for ways they are working around your intended offerings to see how to grow new revenue streams.

2. Ask Why and Listen to the Whole Story. Although frontline staff or call center representatives are busy with core responsibilities, consider ways to encourage your customer-facing staff to elicit detailed personal stories from customers. Whenever possible, ask why they chose your hotel, restaurant, etc., and genuinely show interest in the answers. All the data-mining in the world wouldn't get you to the fact that a family of four sisters always purchased a white Chevy because it's what their grandmother always had and it's a way they like to keep her memory alive. Whirlpool Corporation may never have realized the actual consumer value of their Kitchen Aid mixers until they asked customers to share detailed stories or closely observed how they use the products. At some point they discovered that in many families these mixers are included as a bequest in wills to pass down to younger generations. They originally thought they were making a functional kitchen appliance when in fact they were offering a cherished family asset.

3. Uncovering Sacrifices. In addition to asking for stories, implement systems that allow staff to observe or understand ways customers are making sacrifices or even suffering while attempting to have a great relationship with a business. There are often unintended ways we force customers to make sacrifices or suffer. Whether it be having to wait weeks for an appointment, a complex return policy, unclear terms of sale, or even no way to talk to a real person for a question, never pass up an opportunity to learn more about how the best laid plans to delight may fuel disappointment or even anger.

One of the best—or really, worst—examples of how company procedures cause customer sacrifice or suffering is what happened when a family walked in to pay their hospital bill. In order to reduce expenses, the Cashier's Office of a hospital reduced hours from 8-6 to 8-3. Finance leaders did research and discovered that the number of customers paying bills after 3pm were typically less than 5 a day, making it an optimal place to reduce hours. While this type of efficiency thinking makes sense, extra time to understand and plan ahead for customer impact is required. The new cashier hours were not widely communicated, and two weeks after the change of hours an Amish family had friends drive them 45 minutes into the city to pay their bill. They arrived at the front desk at 4pm and asked for directions to the Cashier Office. The receptionist was cheerful and gave very clear directions, but didn't know about the change in hours. The family walked the long hallways to the Cashier window only to find they closed at 3. They made their way back to the front desk and explained what they found. The cheerful receptionist was confused and sincerely apologized, and the husband then showed her a brown paper bag with $17,000 cash to pay off their bill and asked who could take it. Having no training on this situation, the receptionist told them they would need to come back, and sent them home with their cash in tow. Stories like this happen in most companies without leaders ever knowing that customer sacrifice and suffering is an unintended consequence of prudent operational decisions. The couple did come back the next morning at 8:30 am to get their PAID IN FULL receipt, but it still remained a prime example of customer sacrifice.

"The big idea for Zappos came from little more than the observation of a frustrated customer."

— Joseph Michelli

4. Scan the Sentiments. The "no more secrets" conditions now in place as customer feedback comes fast and furious from many directions can be overwhelming but it's also an opportunity to keep a finger on the pulse of general sentiments of customers or potential customers. It may not be as formal as a customer survey or sales reports, but the flow of social media comments allows a regular check in on sentiment. Having customer-centered staff scan and summarize customer conversations to identify whether things are generally good or generally bad is another way to better understand customer insights. There are also software options that can scan the comments and synthesize what's going well or what isn't to assist with ongoing customer experience issues.

5. Dig Deeper When You are Your Own Customer. In many businesses, the workers can also be the customers. Sometimes the hotel staff actually stay at their hotel, nurses are admitted to the hospital where they work, factory workers buy the cereal they package every day. Insider insights can allow for deeper and wider feedback gathering since these special customers have unique motivation to look at details others may miss. Encourage staff to look deeper and reward their efforts to provide new perspectives on where you are not meeting expectations.

6. Check the General Attitude Toward Trusting Customers. Having some distrust of customers is often subtle, but can be destructive to long-term success. There will likely always be an element of your customer base who try to "game the system" and take more than their share, but that minority of untrustworthy customers shouldn't be driving customer engagement strategies. We've all had an experience where rules or systems seem to tell us that we're untrustworthy, and that's not a loyalty builder. In their book, Smart Trust, Stephen M. R. Covey and Greg Link talk about aligning companies to be "enabled to operate with high trust in a low-trust world by minimizing risk and maximizing possibilities." Companies should consider doing a TRUSTING ATTITUDE AUDIT to see the tone that is used when communicating to customers, policies in place to keep customers in line, and policies that impact the level of trust shown to customers. Often an unintended insulting tone of voice surfaces with the tone in signage or ordering instructions. Some that have caught my eye in to-be-unnamed businesses are:

- Free Refills on Same Visit Only

- Children Cannot be Unattended at Any Time

- Do Not Touch Any Products on Display

- Do Not Take Any of Our Magazines from This Room

One gift we must always try to offer customers is the gift of trust.

7. Work to Predict Perfection. Whenever customers give the gift of candid feedback, incorporate the lessons into an ongoing learning stream for the organization. When customers share ways you've exceeded their expectations and delighted them, log what contributed to this response. Common categories will begin to surface and you will start to see some "sure-thing" strategies you can reliably deploy to better predict almost perfect experiences. Most companies know the likely pain points customers face however, continue to categorize the negative experiences and promote shared learning on what to avoid at all costs. Many studies have shown that negative experiences have much greater impact on the overall experience, so shared learning on how to prevent them is another important way to prepare the organization to better predict near perfect experiences.

8. Dig Deeper to Understand What's Relevant. In addition to accessibility, a good price and good quality, it's important to understand all the ways your offerings are, or can, be relevant to customers. The more needs you can address the more relevant you are to the customer and the more likely you'll beat out others with similar offerings. Authors of the book, *The Experience Economy*, Joe Pine and Jim Gilmore developed the a Progression of Economic Value model that stresses the importance of being relevant to customers. One example they use is why people may choose to celebrate a birthday party at Chuck E. Cheese instead of just baking a cake at home. When you look at levels of relevancy, Chuck E. Cheese offers a cake within the experience but a whole lot more. As a Mom who has been a customer, other relevant aspects of this birthday experience were that: I could invite more people than would be comfortable at my home; I didn't have to clean up a big mess at home; and, there would be many more activities to keep the kids happy. Chuck E. Cheese offered many levels of relevancy for me which made it easy for me to choose their offerings over others.

9. Genuinely Thank Them and Let Them Know What Will Happen Next. However customer feedback finds it's way to your frontline or management staff, be sure to have procedures in place so customers who give the gift of feedback are affirmed for doing so. To close the loop, give staff instructions on what to tell customers happens to the feedback after received. My favorite credit card company is Discover partly because of the cash-back perk, but mostly because of how painless and pleasant the call center interactions have been… every single time. I've had the same bright orange discover card in my wallet for over a decade and recently I unexpectedly received a new card in the mail and instructions about how more secure the new card is. I certainly appreciated the security upgrade but they sent me a pale gray card. They didn't realize that the bright orange card was important for me to find the card and use it regularly in the dark black pit of junk in my purse. I called the call center to ask if they could send me another card that was bright orange and the operator reported sadly there were no orange cards, (that seemed odd since it's their logo color). She shared with me all the other colors she could send and there was one lime green option that I thought might stand out as I tried to avoid spending 15 minutes looking for the card at every store. She probed a bit about why I wanted a bright colored card and I explained it was truly a time saver for me. She affirmed she too had similar issues with her purse. She thanked me for offering that tip and said she was writing up my comments and they would be sent to the customer service management team that day. I was a bit sad to have to switch to a lime green card but thrilled that some executives at Discover would learn from little old me that perhaps card color could connect to spending!

"The primary strategic battle, in virtually any industry you can name, will be the battle to see who can go the farthest in empowering customers. This includes: information access, decision-making, choice, customization and perception of control and ownership."

— Tom Peters

Chapter III
Key Learning Moments I Want to Act Upon:

———————————————

IV

Thoughtful Co-Created Experiences

As you prepare to unleash a force of moment masters, it's crucial to begin with a commitment to being customer driven, customer friendly, customer sensitive, and customer passionate. In addition, the organizational culture must appreciate the small things that lead to big impact. Focusing on achieving the best for customers, one moment at a time is the foundation of a Chief Moment Officer culture.

There are many small things that have become acceptable and lead to mediocre experiences. They are things we walk by each day. Making changes to some of these things will take commitment and some bravery. One act of of brave customer service commitment happened some years ago at the Cleveland Clinic. A common practice at hospitals around the country is that physicians get the best parking spots on property. They have busy schedules, they have to arrive early in the morning or sometimes in a rush, and they're very important members of the team. That thinking made sense for decades. There's one thing the physicians aren't... they aren't sick, aren't having difficulty walking, and they aren't scared as they approach the hospital each day. (Let's hope not). When attending their annual Innovation and Empathy conference I heard from clinical staff how Toby Cosgrove, MD, President of the Cleveland Clinic, took a courageous step to master future moments by changing the parking policies so that patients had the most convenient parking spots. That policy change may have caused great dissatisfaction for some customers and staff but was ultimately the right thing to do for the customer in need. Think about norms in your industry that may be in the way of your primary customer's needs.

WHY DOESN'T "EXCEPTIONAL" HAPPEN MOST OF THE TIME?

Although there are many high performing customer focused companies, (one of my favorites is Overstock.com since every purchase I make is easy and fast), it's very common that we regularly face mediocre or down-right terrible experiences in a typical week. I have found a few key contributing factors in my observations and interviews with leaders and frontline staff in diverse businesses. They are:

1. Staff Don't Consistently Understand Everyone Is In the Customer Service Business. In their book, *Outside In*, Harley Maning and Kenny Bodine of Forester Research state that customer experiences, "Require a new way to manage, looking deep into every process and incentive to see whether it supports the overall goal. If only the C-suite embraces the goal in all dimensions, mediocrity is sure to follow."

2. Teams Not Seeing a Connection Between Their Actions and Customer Reactions. When staff can't clearly connect the dots between their choices on how to respond, how accurately they perform or a general helpful attitude, they won't have an ongoing drive to continually contribute at higher levels.

3. The Entire Organization Doesn't Hear Customers Well. Most businesses believe they have the voice of the customer well monitored and translated throughout the company. Much time is spent on collecting, reporting and synthesizing customer preferences and complaints, however it's wise to regularly check the actual value of what's being collected and shared. Check to see if customer input is untimely, incomplete, confusing, or not clearly communicated and tied to changes that can be made.

4. An Environment of Distractions. If typical workdays in a company rarely allows workers to be fully present, it's easy to forget to attend to big and small customer needs. Whether it's the rush to get 12 patients ready for outpatient surgery, the stress of 225 people who just had their flight cancelled or the constant distraction of security alarms, a constant flow of distractions can push customer needs far down on the list.

5. Lack of Ownership. Not all companies have stock for their employees and not all companies who issue employee stock purchases have teams who behave like owners. Workers need to have a solid sense of ownership of the company and of the customer's satisfaction. One of the best ways to build this connection is to keep staff well informed of the current and future states of the company. Access to insider information builds a sense of importance and trust to help boost commitment.

THE PURSUIT OF THOUGHTFUL CO-CREATION APPROACHES

The following are some concepts that are building blocks to master the power of moments.

1. Co-Creation Commitment. Looking at the organization to identify ways that procedures can be more customer-oriented is a first big step. Next comes the commitment to the co-creation of extraordinary experiences. Often when managers get excited about a new customer service effort, they may go away for training or a retreat to identify ideas to try. This is not a sustainable approach when it comes to extraordinary measures. Philip Newbold, CEO of Memorial Hospital and Health System in South Bend, Indiana shared a common practice back in the 1970's where hospital administrators would work to develop a new Mammography Center and believed they were striving for a great offering. The big misstep was that the leaders at the table were all white men over the age of 30. Although this group had the responsibility and resources to develop such a program, they certainly didn't have the rich and crucial perspectives of women needing an exceptional breast health experience. Having a group of leaders design what they think will be an exceptional experience and then handing it to the customer-facing team to implement doesn't respect the knowledge and lens of the team or the future customers. It's also unlikely that people who had no say in what may delight a customer should be simply directed, with leaders expecting they will follow those directions with joy and enthusiasm. Co-created experiences allow the organization to benefit from the rich insights of those who see the customer from many different perspectives. In their book, *The Power of Co-Creation*, Venkat Ramaswamy and Francis Gouillart explain, "Co-creation draws innovative ideas from customers, employees and stakeholders at large. It increases the capacity of firms to generate insights and take advantage of opportunities they might not have identified, while reducing risk and capital needs." Companies should consider three important stages to build support for the concept of blending the bird's eye and the worm's eye views:

Co-Design　　　　　Co-Creation　　　　　Co-Delivery

It's important to benefit from various internal and external views when initially creating the design promises and parameters for your customers. This Co-Design phase allows businesses to tap into the expertise and lessons learned by those closest to the customer. Owners and leaders should establish the initial scope and objectives and then enhance the foundation with input from team members at all levels. Once the general direction and parameters for an offering are in place, further refinement and creation of the actual experience will benefit from a Co-Creation phase where those who will ultimately face the customers and deliver the experience assist in crafting the words, policies, procedures, menus, product mix, etc. Lastly, when products or services are ready for consumption, how they are delivered and distributed to customers should also be built with a collaborative approach. All three of these collaborative approaches to business offer great enhancements to customer experiences while significantly engaging the staff to feel a sense of ownership as their input is valued along the way.

"I want employees to be in a growth attitude so that they experiment. They have to always be taking a risk."

— Shelly Lazarus

2. Understand and Work Hard at Authenticity. In their book, <u>Authenticity</u>, experience thought leaders Joe Pine and Jim Gilmore state the compelling case that consumers are increasingly discerning how real your offerings are, and that their purchasing decisions are influenced by if they *feel* it's authentic. They state, "Too many companies say they're offering *experiences* without actually *staging* experiences. Now, more than ever, the authentic is what consumers really want." One of the delicate issues in grooming Chief Moment Officers is helping staff conquer opportunities to delight a customer, not behave as mouthpieces of a message they don't even believe themselves. Insincerity or robotic reverence can be spotted by most consumers in seconds. The commitment to co-creation helps engage staff at all levels to offering authentic care and attention to customer needs however, another important step is that they see managers or leaders as role models of authenticity. The relationship between leaders and the rest of the organization must be as transparent as possible, and there needs to be genuine sense of caring. This is easier to achieve in a small business compared to a billion dollar enterprise but the goal should still be pursued. For example, DuPont Corporation is a global manufacturer of thousands of materials and chemicals that touch all of our lives. With a workforce spread across the world, it's a tall order to build a genuine sense of caring. However, they have an unprecedented commitment to worker safety that builds a sense of authentic care. For decades, leaders have upheld core value safety learning at the beginning of every meeting, in person or on the phone. Daily safety lessons are shared, including lessons to help staff be safer at home with their families. Your culture may be driven by other topics but be sure that you work at authentic care for each associate as an important step toward the staging and delivering of authentic customer experiences. The theory here is that those who feel well cared for are much more likely to care well for the customer.

3. Stretch the Aspirations. There are companies that develop annual goals to meet the expectations of their customers and that's a direct path to good old-fashioned mediocrity. More advanced companies strive to exceed customer expectations which moves to the Great zone. As you consider the power of dynamic, memorable moments, your organization should stretch to exceed customer imagination. This can move you to the Outstanding zone. Staging experiences that are Outstanding allows your business to stand out from the competition, stand out in the mind of each consumer, and stand out when it's time for a repeat purchase. In order to exceed imagination, you can't just rely on the customer to share their desires. Deploy innovative solution-seeking tools to stretch staff thinking and find ways to meet needs the customer doesn't realize exist, and work with the staff to uncover requests or behaviors that have never been part of your offerings.

One of the workshops I led years ago included owners of a variety of businesses. One was an auto dealership owner. As I shared a variety of exceptional experience theories and stories, I wasn't sure how much would actually be applied. A year later I ran into the owner of the local Ford-Toyota dealership, and he made a special effort to thank me for the thought-provoking session on customer experiences. He went on to tell me how they had been recognized nationally for what they tried and grew their service revenues. When I asked about some of the concepts that worked, he shared one of the best examples ever of moving from exceeding customer expectations to exceeding customer imagination. We all expect a safe, warm place to sit while our car is being repaired, and we may expect free coffee, tea and water, a TV to watch and perhaps a magazine or two. These are meet expectations efforts. However, this dealership decided first to exceed these expectations by offering private seating where you can work quietly, soft seating, hard-backed seating, an abundant variety of interesting magazines and newspapers, complimentary coffee, tea, water, and cookies, and regular updates from staff on the status of your car repairs. These were the exceed expectations efforts. Then they went one step further. At this dealership, they added a special choice for customers. While waiting for your car, you have the choice of a complimentary chair massage or manicure! These uncommon and unexpected perks definitely exceed customer imagination. These changes also led me to switch companies for my auto service and I thoroughly enjoyed my massages!

4. Appeal to the Heart and the Head. When seeking to align 10 to 10,000 staff members within a business, it's very common to reach out to influence behaviors by sharing facts and appealing to the intellectual side of the workforce. Facts and figures are important however, when you can engage both the head and the heart, understanding grows, commitment grows and empathy grows. In his book, *Eight Habits of the Heart*, Clifton Taulbert outlines values that can build strong communities. As I read his perspective I saw great alignment in some of the habits helping to build strong customer focused businesses as well. The first five habits involve a heart and head connection and this approach works as you engage the workforce to serve, and to engage customers in hopefully a long-term relationship with your business. They are:

A Nurturing Attitude – having a workforce that maintains a nurturing attitude is a priceless customer connecting strength.

Dependability – when customers can depend upon great care and service no matter where they connect with a company, raving fans are born.

Responsibility – living up to promises and taking ownership of missteps is a responsible way to run a business and when everyone honors high levels of responsibility, exceptional experiences are possible.

Friendship – when customers feel like they "have a friend in the business" they feel great confidence around honest answers, great responsiveness and high value. It's not exactly the same as a personal friendship but a spirit of friendship between company representatives and customers supports a Chief Moment Officer culture.

High Expectations – in companies we need to hold one another accountable for having high expectations on how we meet the needs of our customers and exceed their imaginations. We also need not to be afraid of our customers having high expectations of us. When we stay in close touch with changing trends and expectations we can anticipate new ways to stay relevant and embrace high expectations.

"Advertising is the price you pay for being unremarkable."
— Robert Stephens

5. Encourage Empathy and Curiosity. Some people are naturally empathetic and intuitive when engaging with others. One of the best ways to connect with a customer is to be empathetic about where they are in their journey. You can begin an empathetic connection by being curious about customer sacrifices and the stones in their shoes. This can often lead to a more open discussion but also offers a view of new solutions the company could provide. Scan your teams to identify who the highly empathetic individuals are. You'll know them by observing how attentive they are toward customers and co-workers, and how they respectfully probe to get to know people and their needs. Place them in positions of influence where their approaches can be modeled for others. Common sense says the more you know about your customer the better you will be able to exceed their expectations. A good way to act upon that theory is another theory: *the more you look, the more you'll find*. Curiosity with empathy is a perfect approach to look more and find more ways delight your customers.

In his book, *Wired to Care*, Dev Patnaik explains the importance of natural empathetic curiosity. "Our brains have developed subtle and sophisticated ways to understand what other people are thinking and feeling. Simply put, we're wired to care." He promotes the need for companies to build shared intuition: "Organizations should have the gut-level intuition to see how their actions impact the people who matter most: the folks who buy their products, interact with their brand, and ultimately fund their 401(k) plans." Empathy can grow in any company when staff members at all levels are encouraged to not only see the offerings through the eyes of the customers or donors or patients, but also through the heart-mind-skin-nose-stomach of each customer. It's easy to overlook unusual ways your brand, product, or service strikes different types of customers. New aspects of empathy can evolve as teams dig deeper on what customers feel and experience. You can also build empathy and curiosity competencies by sharing stories of great insight gathering and helping others understand ways to become more comfortable engaging with customers if it doesn't come naturally.

On the site www.randomactsofkindness.org, the organizers explain how kindness is teachable and contagious. They include review of some scientific perspectives on the value of kindness including a quote from Dr. Ritchie Davidson from the University of Wisconsin who stated, "It's kind of like weight training, we found that people can actually build up their compassion 'muscle' and respond to others' suffering with care and a desire to help." If you want to build empathy within your company culture, consider ways to build a compassionate team to strengthen the impact of your Chief Moment Officers.

"There's one rule for giving a compliment. The compliment must come from a place of honest gratitude."

— James Rapson and Craig English

6. Common Sense Factor. There is a unique characteristic that must be present to build a force of Chief Moment Officers and it is Common Sense. Former Chief Veteran's Experience Officer Thomas Allin, who was appointed in 2015 to intervene after the national outcry about VA hospital service failures, coined a phrase I believe applies to every company pursing excellence in customer service. He talks about the need for the "Courage of Common Sense." We've all been victims of poor service when common sense is missing from an organization. In order to move from ordinary to extraordinary and be worthy of customer endorsements, courage is needed to see and change whatever is in place that is less than delightful, or even downright awful. It's so easy to walk by the policies or behaviors that seem to suit our staff or technology but may not be suiting our clients. Every business can improve by applying the *Courage of Common Sense* by performing regular "stupidity checks." Having internal staff or external consultants with fresh eyes take a new look at customer touch points to ask WHY whenever something makes life more difficult, less intuitive, more cumbersome for customers. A customer centered enterprise will have the courage to continually look at how they're operating and encourage workers to be courageous to fix things that can negatively impact the overall experience.

7. Consistency Counts. Regardless of the different ways a customer may interact or transact with a company (in person, on the phone, online, via text), it's important to look at all points of contact to insure the experience is consistent in tone, relevancy and energy. Customer-facing expectations and aspirations need to be aligned throughout a company. If not, instead of a reliable customer care culture, a collection of sub-cultures will develop which can confuse customers. Consider refining the expectations with all staff around what every customer should be able to count on whenever they interact with the company. This may include the basics such as que times, return policies, welcome greetings, form design, service recovery, pricing transparency, etc. When consistency is woven into the overall customer service strategy, it helps businesses avoid volatile customer satisfaction scores and fuels customer loyalty.

"Customers want to do business with people they can relate to and companies they admire."

— Harry M. Jansen Kraemer, Jr.

MAKE EXPERIENCE PROMISES AND HAVE STAFF HELP BRING THEM TO LIFE

I had the privilege to be a client of the design innovation company IDEO and one of the most important lessons I learned while working with the talented IDEO teams was the clarifying power of establishing design principles or customer experience promises that will align people, systems and decision-making. An example of a customer experience promise principle within a medical practice could be that we want NO LOST LAMBS... meaning we never want one of our customers to feel lost while interacting with our organization—never lost physically, never lost about steps in the process, never lost about what to wear, never lost about payment expectations, never lost in their understanding of the diagnostic or treatment options. If this was adopted as a design principle in a physician practice, all staff could then be engaged to deliver upon this promise. This guiding principle would be a priority throughout the operation by involving staff at all levels to offer input on how to reliably insure customers or patients never feel lost. This approach would be one foundation of a co-created experience plan. Examples of how NO LOST LAMBS could come to life in a medical group might be:

1. Clear website content with pre-visit instructions, new patient profile forms, directions for parking, insurance plans accepted, etc.

2. There would be "greeters" at all public entrances to guide patients and family to their destinations as well as clear and effective signage or directional kiosks throughout the building.

3. Nurses would have exam room checklists that include a step by step overview of what the patient can expect will happen during their visit, who they will see (XRay Tech, Physician, Physical Therapist, etc.), how much time each step is likely to take and what specific tests they will have and why... etc, etc.

One clear customer design promise or principle can build needed synergy toward a reliably delightful experience and shared understanding of what a team of Chief Moment Officers should prioritize.

Chapter IV
Key Learning Moments I Want to Act Upon:

————————————————

V

Chief Moment Officer Truths to Try

Seeds Don't Blossom in Bad Soil. Chief Moment Officers must live within a culture that celebrates, tolerates, and facilitates staff reaching out anticipate needs, right wrongs, prevent customer suffering, and color outside the lines to give the gift of a delightful moment. One way to prepare the ground for the planting of delightful experience seeds is to remember to connect the dots between the WHY behind customer experience approaches and the HOW. Many companies dwell only on the HOW or WHAT they want staff to do but regularly explaining the reasons these actions are important helps staff feel better connected to the strategy and reduces the need for some second-guessing. Leaders must enthusiastically and consistently connect these dots to support a rich experience culture.

Interview Applicants Using Some New Questions. When screening applicants to enter your organization, consider adding in a few new and unexpected questions to the process. Two to consider are:

- Can you share some of your favorite ways in your personal or professional life you try to make others feel special?

- In your past positions, what would your former supervisors or colleagues say they remember most about your positve impact on the customer experience?

Candidates who enthusiastically jump right in and offer many examples are likely ones you want to pursue. Those who struggle or seem to need more time to come up with an answer may not be best prepared to reliably create exceptional moments for your customers.

Unleashing the Power within Each Person. In addition to the power of titles and words, there is unexpected power in committing to have fun with this process. Engaging staff in traditional boring, one-way, you-listen-we-train programs won't offer memorable or meaningful reasons to change one's view of the world. The time and energy spent building the foundation for a grand new customer-centric culture should be unexpectedly fresh, fun and inviting. Design highly interactive customer experience training sessions that are unlike other typical meetings, the content and approach should allow everyone at any level to feel able to contribute and understand the desired destination. Be sure to create a safe environment where insights large and small can be shared and woven into future strategies. In order to reduce the chance of mediocre contributions, offer a clear framework of priority behaviors. The more you create experiences that delight your staff, the more they'll connect with how powerful this can be for others.

Shared Learning and Buzz Building. Create a Moments Museum. As great customer experience approaches are launched within your organization, it's important to share that knowledge and encourage others to try what's worked within the organization. Consider creating a visible space—I've called mine the Masterpiece Moments Museum—and encourage team members to display their customer delight efforts for others to learn from. The existence of this unexpected display will build buzz in the organization, will help recognize the risk-taking and successful efforts, and continue to support shared learning.

Remember the Foundations of Serving Customers. There are many interesting perspectives to consider as outlined in the previous chapters, however there are some basic principles to remember: Fulfill promises as stated; Be on time; Fix mistakes promptly; Show appreciation whenever you can; Strive to delight through positive emotional connections. Also, strive to prompt the emotions that all of us desire to feel: Special; At Ease; Satisfied; Safe; Fun; Important; Appreciated; Worthy and Confident.

Be diligent about not prompting negative emotions none of us expect to feel: Disrespect; Frustration; Optional; Burdensome; Unnoticed; Stupid; or Trivial.

 Chief Moment Officers are Born and Raised. There are absolutely some personality types who are naturally born Chief Moment Officers. These are people who aim to please other most of the time and who are generally caring, cheery souls. However, they too need a framework for how to most effectively connect with customers and in some cases not go too far. Other personality types need to have the dots connected for them on how to take what might be a desire in their heart and mind and turn into actionable, repeatable steps they can feel comfortable doing on a regular basis. There's a third group that are typically task oriented, less people oriented and they need the benefits, short and long term, of Chief Moment Officer activities to be spelled out and explained. They may need an actual outline to follow to help them see how one delightful moment at a time adds up to company strength and job security. The last group is a group that wants their paycheck, wants to show up and be part of something, but also wants to do as little as possible. They may not particularly care for people other than their personal connections and they don't like to be told by others how to act or react. These people are hard to convert over to the CMO role and when identified should be invited to work for your competitor or given extra exposure to the tools and objectives.

 What's Inside Counts Most. The true power of the Chief Moment Officer is the intrinsic affirmation this stirs up in some staff members. Many frontline staff will report they feel basically powerless within their job and that policies and procedures set by people they've never met are part of what they struggle with on a daily basis. They may also feel helpless to suggest changes or explain problems some of these policies and procedures cause for the front line. When an organization authentically reaches out to those closest to the customer to share perspectives on new ways to delight the customer, and when the staff members feel their contributions are valued and acknowledged, they get the gift of a new sense of power. Initially it may be a quick rush of confidence or enthusiasm, but as they test the waters in the future and see that new approaches were incorporated into some improvements, this move from powerless to powerful fuels cultural change. Everything looks better when you feel you actually can make a difference.

 Encourage Courage. There are times when delighting customers will require some amount of courage. Courage may involve having the guts to speak up when someone is upset and needs information they don't have, or it may involve accommodating a need or desire outside the usual and customary operations. Although all acts of courage may not delight the owners or company management, staff who have the courage to try to delight customers need to be supported. Whenever possible, reward acts of courageous customer support even if the ultimate outcome is not perfect. Stories will be shared over the years about courageous attempts and how the company embraced the wins and the diligent attempts!

One of the most touching stories of customer service courage I observed was in a physician's office. This was a high-risk obstetrics practice and patients visited the office to understand the diagnosis of high risk conditions and then were typically followed throughout their pregnancies. A 22-year-old had recently been hired as the office receptionist and had only been in her new exciting first job for 3 months. She had been through some of our immersive experience design workshops when she was hired but we hadn't exactly planned for this situation. One day when the practice waiting room was filled with expectant parents, a couple was being seen in one of the exam rooms for their initial diagnosis. The physician and nurse needed to share the news that their baby would be born with Spina Bifida, a congenital spine disorder. This was a shocking surprise to the couple and the medical experts were attempting to share a plan of care with the couple. However, the pregnant mother was so distraught at the news, she was inconsolable. She sobbed for over 20 minutes and with other patients waiting, the physician asked that they take some time to process the information and they would follow up on the phone the next day. Other patients couldn't help but hear the emotional reaction and after another 15 minutes the nurse and husband were able to encourage the expectant Mom to head home. As they made their way to the waiting room, the new receptionist decided to use her courage muscle. She stood up from her desk, walked over to the couple with a slight limp and softly said, "I heard about your news today and I wanted to let you know that I have Spina Bifida and it may not be as bad as you think... I graduated high school and I now have this great new job and my doctors have helped me do well." With this touching outreach, the expectant Mom stopped crying and it seemed as if the weight of the world came off her shoulders. She hugged the young receptionist and thanked her again and again for sharing her story. This newly hired employee exceeded the expectations of this couple and her employer. If she hadn't had the courage to stand up and share, unnecessary customer suffering could have continued. It's likely that nothing the nurse and doctor could have shared would have been as powerful as the receptionist's example. Encouraging acts of courage such as speaking up when you may be able to make a difference helps support a customer passionate business.

Wrappings Matter. Some feel what's inside the gift box is all that matters, but I hope you won't underestimate the power of the wrapping. In this case, the wrapping is the job of C.M.O. If some type of prestigious and respected credentials are offered to team members who may have never imagined they would be honored and celebrated in this way, I've seen teams respond with true excitement and pride. Establishing some type of credibility or expert designations that connect the training and expectations to each individual's view of their role and their potential is an important step toward sustainable cultural commitments to exceptional experiences. Enhancing one's view of oneself may lead to enhancement of one's view of what they can contribute toward the greater good. Consider official designations and visible celebration of learning as staff are trained and begin to apply customer experience enhancements.

"Customers Can Never Be an Inconvenience."

— Diane S. Hopkins

 Walking the Talk. This is crucial when launching an exceptional experience journey to build a workforce of Chief Moment Officers. Before expectations, scripts, or procedures can be well understood and digested, your team should FEEL the difference themselves. They need to benefit from an exceptional experience in being invited to participate in learning or ideation activities, they need to feel more welcomed than ever before, they need to feel their personal needs were met whenever possible such as with seating options, food and refreshment options, learning styles, and more. They need to see senior leaders as servant leaders interested in them and excited to get to know them and their perspective better. Be sure that the staff will be delighted by the experience they have as you prepare to expand your approach to delighting your customers. Their memory of how they were treated, surprised, and valued in meetings, training or routine communications will help all of the future expectations for customers ring true and make sense for years to come.

Pride is Priceless. A sense of pride about our jobs, careers, or vocations is not something that can be valued on a balance statement, but it is an asset worth more than we could ever count. We've all been at a restaurant and experienced the difference between a server who has pride in every contact we have with their establishment and those who could care less and want to be done with the needs of each table as quickly as possible. The unleashing of Chief Moment Officers is as much a customer service strategy as it is a pride-building and protecting strategy. No matter what the industry, pride-filled teams have good energy, hearts in the right place, and actions to match. Pride is a bit like your future. You can sit back and see how it unfolds on its own, or you can deliberately and thoughtfully nurture it and help it blossom, one person or department at a time. Take time to think about your pride-building plan for the next year. Consider committing to a bold prideful event or effort every month involving the entire company.

 Build a Team of Boasters. One way to help new customers feel they've made the right choice when choosing your offering is to prepare your team members to gush about the company. Waiters have to have tasted menu items to be able to recommend their favorite items when customers ask what's a good choice. Whether you're in a Business to Business company or Business to Consumer company, staff must have a detailed understanding of what makes the company great now and in the past and be encouraged to authentically share that information with customers. Boasting or bragging is often looked down upon unless it's about your kids or grandkids. In this case, think about the power of having all your staff truthfully and respectfully boasting about the company offerings as a way to build customer confidence. Enthusiastic bragging can help prepare customers to enjoy their experience.

Person by Person Promises. As workers are oriented or trained to focus on customers, the old adage, "You Never Get a Second Chance to Make a First Impression" holds true for all of us. As you share the overall company vision on how to serve the customer, think about assigning each staff member to create their own personal vision statement on how they will create first, last and lasting impressions for the customers they serve. If everyone creates their own Personal Customer-Pleasing Promise that aligns with the overall company vision, you blend the best of the individuals and the whole. This helps avoid the "Do as We Say" directive approach to customer service and celebrates what each individual brings to the organization. Each short promise statement should be easy to remember and a centering of the attitude, tone, energy and approach that is meaningful to each person. The phrase should be posted in their workspace for others to see and can be refined over the years as they see new ways to delight. You might share some possible examples to get people comfortable with the concept such as:

I AM A PASSIONATE LISTENER
I WILL TALK WITH, NOT TO MY CUSTOMERS
I COMMIT TO DELIGHTING
I CAN MAKE OR BREAK CUSTOMER MOMENTS
I WILL COMPLIMENT EVERY CUSTOMER I MEET
I WILL BE MINDFUL
I WILL NEVER CREATE A RUSHED EXPERIENCE
TODAY I'LL DELIGHT
LIFE IS TOO SHORT FOR MEDIOCRITY
SEEKING RAVING FANS

"Do what you do so well that they will want to experience it again and bring their friends."

— Walt Disney

 Don't Just Ask How Well The Company Is Doing. Almost every company does some type of customer satisfaction research. This can be a very big expense for an organization so it's important to gather not only the traditional feedback but to try to tap into unmet needs. Take time to refresh the customer survey questions to try to build upon expressed needs and desires.

If an auto dealership looks at how they meet time management needs of customers searching for a new car, they may be able add value by probing deeper on other time management solutions they might offer. A Lexus dealer I have used expanded their questions around time management for the car purchase experience as well as car maintenance. They added questions beyond how well service was provided with questions on what customers experienced while shopping and making a purchase. They looked at a variety of time management possibilities and became one of the first to arrange for car titles and registration processing to be completed right there in the dealership. This had been missed as part of the customer journey at most dealerships but when customer satisfaction data is expanded to look for new ways to be more relevant, great experiences can follow.

Sometimes Old is New and Exceptional. With so much of our business and personal purchasing completed online, older customer satisfaction policies may have sometimes been missed in the rush to maximize technology advances. Many online advertisers who seek to promote their companies through search engine optimization and targeted advertising messages can only interact with the web and search companies by sending an email and waiting. This technology driven structure required one thing that customers never like... waiting for hours or day. A few years ago Google enhanced their customer service by launching traditional real-time phone support in over 40 languages as well as video chat. Phone access to Google experts seemed like a revolutionary idea in the age of technology solutions. More and more web-based companies are incorporating ways to talk to a real person as a way to listen and quickly respond to customers. Think about traditional connections to customers you may have turned away from that may need a second chance.

Sometimes Speed is What You Need. In some companies it's not a great product that solves a customer's problem or a wonderfully friendly receptionist that will turn a first-time buyer into a raving fan. Sometimes speeding up the time between the moment a customer decides to buy and fulfilment of the purchase can be the moment they'll never forget. Delivering awesome response times requires alignment of operations rigor and staff priorities at all levels. If this turns out to be a driver of customer delight in your business, the pursuit of speed must always be balanced with quality, safety and other standards toward exceptional moment making.

Hold Onto Praise. As customer compliments come into a business they are typically shared initially with those who are directly tied to the message. One way to balance out days when there are far more complaints than compliments is to re-visit the thank you notes, emails and letters to use as a library of encouragement. Consider developing a WE WERE AWESOME repository of customer praise that leaders and staff can access anytime. These real-life reactions can be used as meeting ice-breakers or shared when orienting new employees.

Technology Solutions need Experience Plans. Although new patient registration software in a physician office, an upgrade to an ATM system or a mobile app for grocery delivery offers enhanced speed or convenience for customers, technology turned on isn't enough to insure a delightful experience. Thoughtfully introduced technology solutions can make a great difference. Be sure to consider the likely needs for successful adoption based on existing customer habits and consider how well integrated the upgrades are with other aspects of the operation to avoid unintended customer frustration. Never purchase and install technology until there's a customer experience impact plan in place.

Easier Workdays for Staff Benefits the Customer. As expected, most customer service interventions focus upon how to make life easier for customers to select your business and purchase your goods or services. Another perspective to consider is the cascading impact of making life easier or simpler for staff which may also make life better for your customers. Processes or policies that are simplified or more efficient can improve staff satisfaction and attitudes. The theory to test here is that if each day is more pleasant for your workforce, that pleasantness may be evident to customers. When staff have less cumbersome steps and less complex repetitive tasks to attend to, they should have more time to attend to customer needs and desires and to create Masterpiece Moments!

Address Negative Customer Sub-Cultures. Most companies automatically approach customer interactions with a positive tone and sense of respect. Managers may not be aware however of the existence of a thriving sub-culture in the company that includes disrespectful frameworks around customer profiles, needs or behaviors. What we think and believe impacts what we say and how we behave. It's important to listen and observe backstage conversations and nomenclature used to describe customers and customer interactions. Seemingly light-hearted, throw away comments about customers may give an indication whether a negative sub-culture exists. Clues to look for are:

- Use of customer nicknames such as: whiners, lazy, hot heads, big mouths, slackers, etc.

- Post customer encounter laughter

- Negative social media posts about work and customer needs

- Complaints about customer requests or desires

- Reduced atmosphere of civility among staff that can rub off on customers

Any of these situations may signal a sub-culture that needs to be addressed to build a customer focused culture. Leaders must be prepared to re-direct these types of behaviors even if they're connected to a stressful work environment and a way staff have learned to let off steam.

Real-Time Re-Direction of Customer Unfriendly Team Members. One important cultural component that supports the Chief Moment Officer approach is that team members feel responsible for stopping one another when failing to treat customers with respect. It must be the norm that when one staff member observes another treating a customer unkindly or unprofessionally, they need to know how and be willing to re-direct in the moment. Of course it can take courage to speak up to a colleague or jump in to a tense situation but it's an important foundation of a CMO strategy to prevent bad behaviors from becoming the norm.

Humor is Humanizing. Although it can be hard to gauge what's fun and funny to one person vs. another, humor can be an effective way to build relationships with customers. Offering a light tone or humorous comment can help accelerate a sense of comfort and familiarity and help to diffuse a tense or confusing situation. Staff need to be sensitive to the difference between lame/negative humor and a light/endearing sense of humor to lighten a moment. Laughter is proven to contribute to an emotional and sometimes physical sense of well-being so why not offer those benefits to your customers from time to time? A side benefit of humor being applied appropriately is that work-life for the staff can also be more enjoyable and less mundane. I recently stopped into a Dollar Tree store and they were only open 45 minutes with one register open and a line of 9 people had already formed. As people were showing impatience with the wait, the cashier continued to work as fast as she could but announced to those of us in line, "This is why we sell razors here. Sometimes before the next cashier arrives you guys will grow beards before you check out." She said it with a fun, light-hearted tone and everyone in line smiled or laughed. I was in a hurry and my anxious feeling disappeared in that moment. It may not have been a corporate approved script but it surely changed the atmosphere for those in line.

Chapter V
Key Learning Moments I Want to Act Upon:

VI

Unleashing Your Inner Chief Moment Officer

Now that you have explored this unique role and how it might lead to enhanced customer experience performance, no matter what your industry, it's a perfect time to begin your personal journey. Since it's impossible to be with all readers for an official CMO celebration ceremony, here are instructions on how to conduct your personal transition toward becoming a Chief Moment Officer:

1. Find a small gift box. First, place one of your very favorite snacks in the box. Then write down your vision of what the Chief Moment Officer philosophy might mean for your career and your organization. Place the paper in the box and stash it away. (Don't forget where you put it).

2. Seven days from today, make a note on your calendar at a perfect time to move to the next step and retrieve your box. (A perfect time is when you know you'll have at least 30 minutes alone).

3. Find a comfortable quiet spot. Take your shoes off and if possible, have some of your favorite music playing. (I have three songs to suggest you play depending upon what's driving your quest to improve your contributions. Although they may seem odd at first, if you play them and truly listen, your Chief Moment Officer ceremony will be enhanced. My recommendations: For those who desire to show their personal impact on improving their organization: One Voice by Barry Manilow. For those who are driven by a desire to build consensus around a better way to operate a company: Extraordinary by Mandy Moore. And, for those who are excited about aligning an organization to get from good to almost perfect: Masterpiece by Andy Grammer. Open your box and begin to enjoy your favorite snack. Then re-read your vision of how being a Chief Moment Officer could have a positive impact. After that, read and sign this next page:

Unleashing My
CHIEF MOMENT OFFICER

"They won't always remember what you said, or what you did, but they will always remember the way you made them feel."

— Maya Angelou

Mastering Moments is a concept I value, and I can see a personal and professional path toward making a remarkable difference for customers I come in contact with and colleagues I influence. There's no better time, no better person to further explore the power of a magnificent, memorable, meaningful, masterpiece moment. I see great possibilities ahead and will continue to develop this perspective and my personal impact.

I pledge to begin this important work as soon as I finish my favorite snack!

Date:_____

Enthusiastically Signed:_____

Please use the initials C.M.O. after your name from this day forward and enthusiastically explain the meaning to all who ask. Wishing you great experimentation and lasting success! Don't stop until the moments you design are Beautiful!

**Diane Serbin Hopkins,
CEE**

Summary and Final Thoughts

Throughout this book the word "customer" has been used as a universal descriptor for those who desire to purchase or affiliate, join or connect to some type of organization or offering. Depending upon your motivation for reading this book, "customer" may need to be replaced by: patient, donor, member, user, client, partner or passenger. Hopefully you've been able to connect your needs to the overall message.

We are all customers and we've all seen the good, bad, exceptional and ugly in how we've been treated in our personal or professional purchasing experiences. Being generic or being acceptable is not a path to long term strength and viability for any company. In his Future Shape of the Winner model, business author Tom Peters talks about TALENT (who we choose to bring into organizations and who we choose to retain), is at the core of finances, engaged staff, customer satisfaction, market relevancy and good citizenship. His model stresses that TALENT is at the center of crucial balancing acts around things like execution, brand and customer experience. We may have our financial, facility and legal resourcing in order, however if our most important human resources aren't well prepared to understand and accommodate customer needs and desires, winning is an unlikely destination.

The pursuit of a company of Chief Moment Officers requires a similar focus and appreciation of TALENT. The balance in the CMO model is between:

CUSTOMER PASSIONATE TALENT **ONGOING CUSTOMER INSIGHTS**

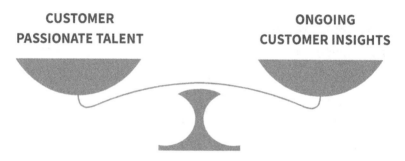

EXCEPTIONAL EXPERIENCE ESSENTIALS

As your organization considers the potential impact the Chief Moment Officer role could have on your existing talent and the ability to recruit new talent, consider that this is a cultural journey not an overnight fix. In order to prepare your teams to embrace this role you can't decree staff to exceed customer expectations. There are unfortunately too many stories of customer service training that focuses on telling staff all they are to do instead of igniting staff insights alongside company aspirations toward mutual rewards. As you've read the previous chapters, some key concepts help define what a Chief Moment Officer strategy requires:

1. Bigger thinking around smaller acts that can build raving fans and that moments matter.

2. A belief that delivering what the customer wants *and* needs is a gift and when customers share their specific dissatisfactions that too is a *gift*.

3. Support of co-creation approaches takes advantage of the knowledge of those who have different views of the customer within your company while showing how each person's input is valued.

4. Ongoing communication and reminders of customer conditions and desires can counter the effects of distracted, busy teams and help them keep the end game in mind.

5. Thoughtful exceptional experiences must be thoughtfully staged, designed or assembled and they aren't likely to be a reliable part of your company otherwise.

6. It's crucial that companies properly orient and influence staff to delight customers whenever possible not as a special training initiative but ultimately as an instinct within the company culture. It's about moving from Directed Actions to Inspired Actions.

7. Companies must cultivate soil that re-engages the workforce to own not only the company but each customer they come in contact with.

8. Planting seeds of competency so that staff can adopt new ways to delight customers and readily share success stories.

9. Modeling exceptional experience strategies not only for customer facing activities but also applying the approaches for the internal customers. Whether it be new employee orientation, rewards events or ongoing staff meetings, be sure to take every opportunity to insure the staff members experience aspects of what you hope they'll bring to the customers.

10. Ongoing celebration and communication of new levels of customer influence wisdom and comfort around promptly sharing customer interaction mistakes.

11. Commitment to spending time on refining intentions of all workers so that customer contacts are never taken for granted. Great intentions don't always delight but they certainly increase the odds.

12. Diligence around influencing all staff to bring their best to the customers by optimizing one on one connections and open discussions about staying relevant to those who keep the company alive.

13. Mixing facts and emotions as Chief Moment Officer approaches are shared. The heart and head connection is crucial in influencing adoption and enhanced performance.

14. Regular coordination and assessments of how the company operates and how operations may impact the customer experience. Things that may make perfect sense for productivity or budgets may backfire and lead to unintended customer consequences.

Reliable exceptional customer experiences are an easy–to–support desire for any organization, but not always an easy strategy to launch. The effort however is worthy not only for the obvious customer relationship strengthening but also to drive employee commitment enhancements. I've seen staff at all levels get excited and passionate about a new-found sense of importance and influence when they were invited to be part of a customer moment effort. Staff can easily feel lost in a company and believe they have little or no significance in the overall enterprise. In addition to enhanced customer relationships, the launching of a *Chief Moment Officer* approach can have many internal benefits when staff discover their personal connection to company success. When that happens on a grand scale, the company wins, the stockholders win, the staff wins and of course the customer wins the gift of exceptional company performance.

Advice from a Chief Moment Officer

As you seek each day to deliver the best,

Remember there are those who see what you don't.

Striving to delight is a pursuit that offers no rest,

Perhaps your team will do it well and your competitors won't.

There are untapped hearts and minds to discover,

There are innovative suggestions ready to try.

You can build a company of customer lovers,

Uninspired *takers* need not apply.

Every worker can make a difference with their words,

effort and care,

Leaders must prepare them to have influence lift.

Never allow your feedback to be that of *Buyer Beware*,

Deliberately make every moment for a customer a gift!

RECOMMENDED ADDITIONAL READING:

Amaze Every Customer Every Time, Shep Hyken

Anxious to Please, James Rapson and Craig English

Authenticity, Joe Pine and Jim Gilmore

Differentiate or Die, Jack Trout and Steve Rivkin

Eight Habits of the Heart, Clifton Taulbert

From Values to Action, Harry M. Jansen Kraemer, Jr.

Magnetic Service, Chip R. Bell and Bilijack R. Bell

Markets of One, Joe Pine and Jim Gilmore

Milkshake Moment, Steven S. Little

Outside In, Harley Manning, Kenny Bodine

Prescription for Excellence, Joseph A. Michelli

Service Fanatics, James Merlino, MD

The Circle of Innovation, Tom Peters

The Customer Comes Second, Hal Rosenbluth

The Effortless Experience, Matthew Dixon and Nick Toman

The Experience Economy, Joe Pine and Jim Gilmore

The Power of Co-Creation, Venkat Ramaswamy and Francis Gouillart

The Starbucks Experience, Joseph A. Michelli

What Customers Want, Anthony W. Ulwick

Wired to Care, Dev Patnaik

www.deliveringhappiness.com, Happiness as a Business Model, Tony Hsieh

www.randomactsofkindness.org

Woo, Wow and Win, Thomas A. Stewart and Patricia O'Connell

IMAGE CREDITS

Page 25: sunshine-91/vecteezy.com, zhaolifang/vecteezy.com

Page 27: kmlmtz66/Shutterstock.com

Page 32, 39, 109 and 116: Designed by Freepik

Diane Serbin (Stover) Hopkins is a Certified Experience Economy Expert and WOW project guru and has been a customer experience practitioner in the services industry for 15 years. She is co-author of the book, Wake Up and Smell the Innovation and has been featured on the PBS special, Re-Imagine Business Excellence with Tom Peters for ways she re-invented the impact marketers can have on the customer experience in the healthcare industry. She has served as an internal consultant and trainer for companies including: Beacon Health, DuPont Corporation, Atlantic Health System, Saint Gobain, Freedom Healthworks, Vynamic and others. She is a frequent speaker at professional conferences throughout the US and faculty member at the Pennsylvania College of Health Science and founding faculty member at IVIA Innovation Mentor Program at the University of Notre Dame. To learn more about Diane's work, visit www.chiefmomentofficer.com

CPSIA information can be obtained
at www.ICGtesting.com
Printed in the USA
LVHW082120020519
616133LV00001B/1/P

9 781944 027223